BRITTANY BUBBLE GUM'S ICKY, STICKY LANDFILL JOURNEY

by Jamee-Marie Edwards illustrated by Christian Cornia

PICTURE WINDOW BOOKS
a capstone imprint

Hi there! My name is Brittany Bubble Gum.

I'm here to share what happens to me after my flavor is gone. I know! It's a sticky job. But someone has to do it. So, hang on. My trip to the **landfill** might get a little bumpy.

At first, my life was everything I dreamed.

Then I ended up in a dark, smelly place called a trash can. I'm stuck to a paper towel. I'm here with a bunch of food scraps. I see an old red balloon over there too.

As I'm trying to settle in . . .

. . . my trash can friends and I are tossed toward the hopper of a garbage truck. ***Thud!*** We land inside. The items in the green and blue bins don't come with us. They will go to a place to be recycled.

Hydraulics push my trash buddies and me into the truck's container. The container is in the middle of the truck. All the trash goes here until the truck is full.

Whirr! A compactor inside the container squishes everything together. It feels like a giant trash sandwich. I'm getting flatter by the second!

Thud! The truck stops to pick up more trash. It makes several stops in the neighborhood.

Finally, our truck is full. Off we go to the landfill.

Out we go, tumbling onto a huge pile of trash. My trash buddies and I will get covered with a layer of dirt. Trash is very stinky. The dirt helps reduce the smell. It also keeps pesky rodents away.

Each day, new trash is added on top of us. My trash buddies and I are getting pressed into thick, tightly packed layers.

By the way, my new home is called a municipal solid waste landfill or MSWLF. Trash from homes, schools, hospitals, and businesses is brought here.

The ground beneath us is lined with clay and plastic. The lining keeps anything icky from leaking into the water below ground.

Sometimes, rainwater flows through the layers of trash. This creates a liquid waste called **leachate**. It is harmful to the environment. Special pipes in the landfill collect the leachate. The leachate gets cleaned before it goes back into nature.

Days turn into weeks.

Today, I woke up stuck to a new, soft and comfy Best Trash Buddy (BTB). My paper towel BTB **biodegraded**. That's when I found out trash in landfills breaks down over time.

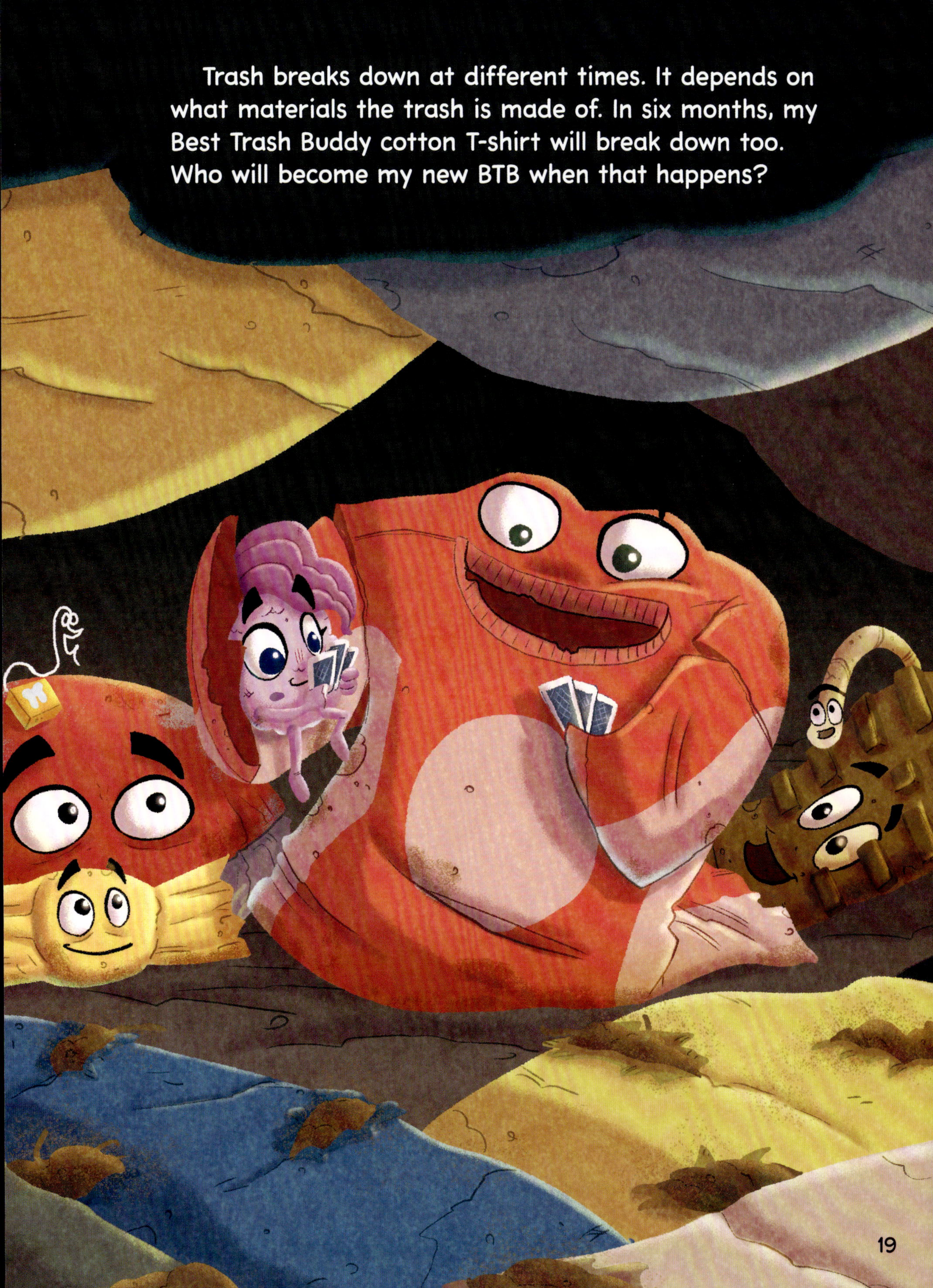
Trash breaks down at different times. It depends on what materials the trash is made of. In six months, my Best Trash Buddy cotton T-shirt will break down too. Who will become my new BTB when that happens?

As for me, I am non-biodegradable. That's a fancy way to say, I stick around for a very long time.

I am made of a material called gum base. Gum base contains **polyethylene** and other materials. Polyethylene does not break down easily like other materials.

I can live in this landfill for hundreds to thousands of years. I will make a lot of BTBs by staying here that long.

Say hello to rope and wool sock, my new buddies.

I'll be here for at least a year.

I'll be here for five years!

The years go by.

For the next 20 years, I will share laughs with this candy wrapper BTB. Her plastic crinkles tickle.

Many trash friends in my layer have disappeared. Some of my trash friends, like the dental floss, have been here for years. The Mylar balloon has been here just as long! Both of them will be here with me for many more years.

Years turn into **decades**.

Today I am 60 years old. I have been stuck to my current Best Trash Buddy for 40 years. Rubber is another material that takes a long time to break down.

Surprise! My trash friends have a party for me. We laugh and share stories.

Things continue to change. More of my trash buddies have broken down. Even my landfill looks different now. Fresh layers of clay and dirt have sealed off parts of it. Grass and small trees grow on top of the soil. Birds and animals visit.

My landfill has turned into a wildlife conservation park.

What a journey this has been! I went from being a party favor to a long-term resident of a landfill. Along the way, I've made a lot of Best Trash Buddies.

I'm proof that even trash has a story to tell. And mine is far from finished.

Remember, next time you throw something in the trash, some of us will be sticking around for many, many years to come!

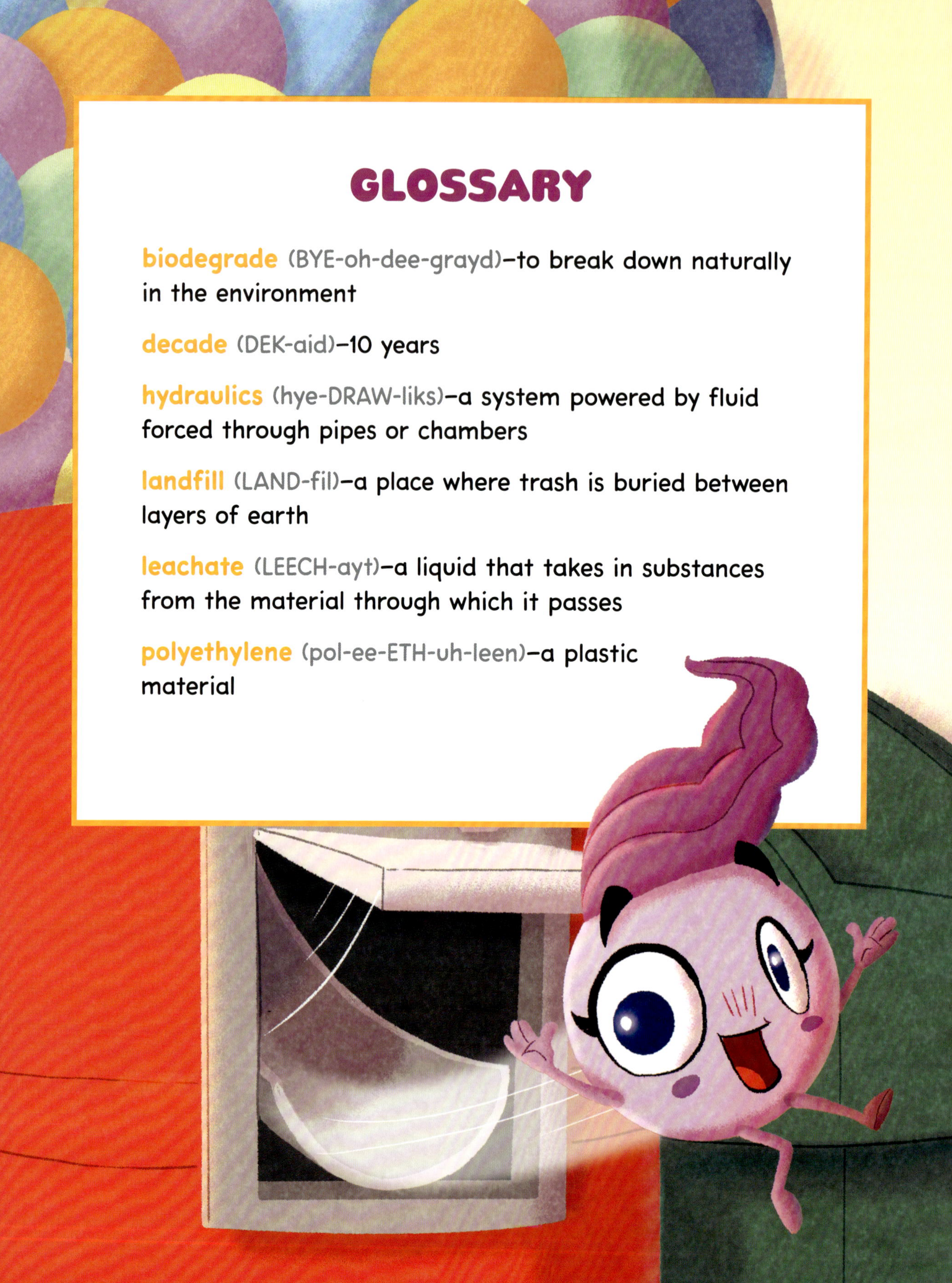

GLOSSARY

biodegrade (BYE-oh-dee-grayd)—to break down naturally in the environment

decade (DEK-aid)—10 years

hydraulics (hye-DRAW-liks)—a system powered by fluid forced through pipes or chambers

landfill (LAND-fil)—a place where trash is buried between layers of earth

leachate (LEECH-ayt)—a liquid that takes in substances from the material through which it passes

polyethylene (pol-ee-ETH-uh-leen)—a plastic material

Photo Credit MaseFX

ABOUT THE AUTHOR

Jamee-Marie Edwards is an author, STEAM educator, and literacy advocate from New York City who is on a mission to ignite imagination and inspire children through creativity and education. Her experience in school health and health education has allowed her to connect with youth on various levels. As the founder of The Me I Need To Be Program, Jamee-Marie creates accessible platforms for learning in which she merges the Arts and Sciences to provide students with the opportunity to express themselves, build confidence, and gain essential skills. Learn more about Jamee-Marie at her website maeinspireu.com

ABOUT THE ILLUSTRATOR

Christian Cornia is a character designer, illustrator, and comic artist from Modena, Italy. At age four, while flipping through a comic book, he decided he wanted to become a comic artist. He has created characters and illustrations for books, advertising, video games, and role-playing games. He has worked as an inker for Marvel. He's also the artist behind the graphic novel series Brina. He collaborates with the international illustration agency Advocate Art and teaches courses at the Reggio Emilia International School of Comics.

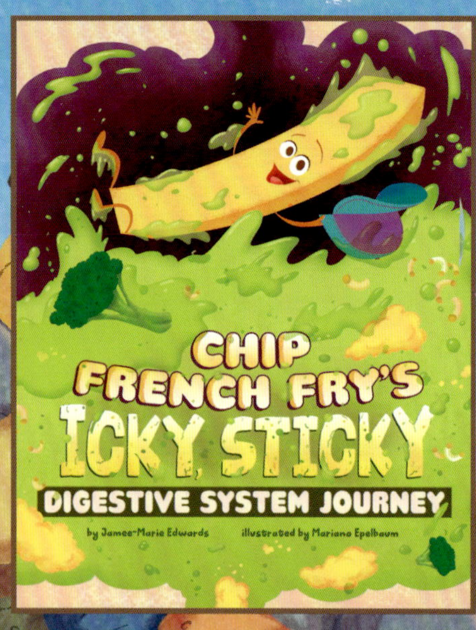

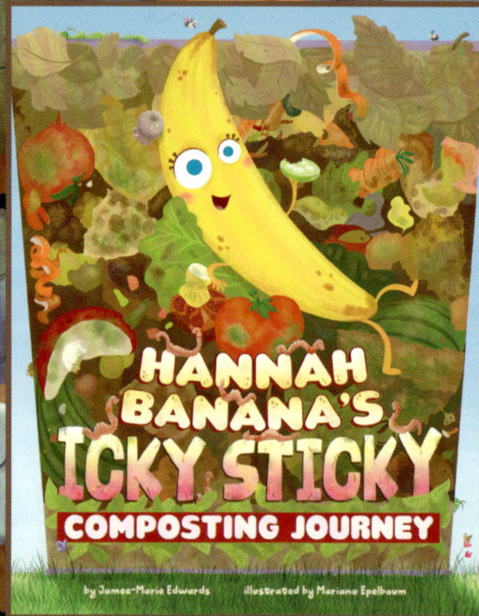

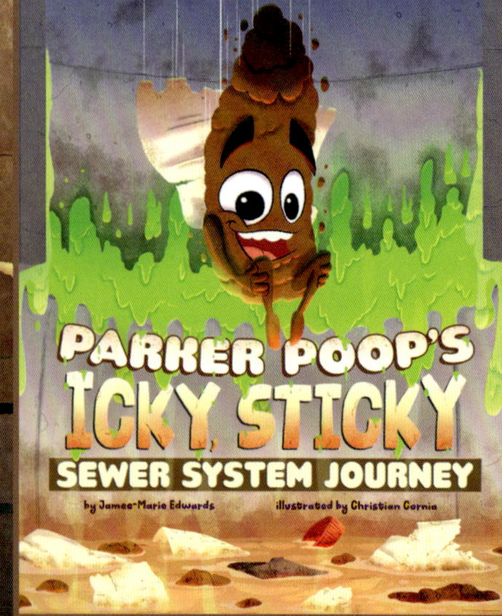

Published by Picture Window Books, an imprint of Capstone
1710 Roe Crest Drive, North Mankato, Minnesota 56003
capstonepub.com

Library of Congress Cataloging-in-Publication Data is available on the Library of Congress website.

ISBN: 9798875238093 (hardcover)
ISBN: 9798875238048 (paperback)
ISBN: 9798875238055 (ebook PDF)

Summary: An illustrated first-person narrative of Brittany Bubble Gum's journey from the trash can to the landfill.

Designer: Hilary Wacholz

Printed and bound in China. 006461